W9-BGU-448

DATE DUE			
He			

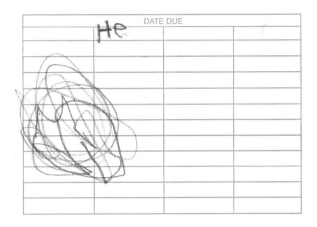

59317

#16. 99

Bugs, Bugs, Bugs!

Grasshoppers

by Margaret Hall

Consulting Editor: Gail Saunders-Smith, PhD

Consultant: Gary A. Dunn, MS, Director of Education
Young Entomologists' Society Inc.
Lansing, Michigan

Capstone
press

Mankato, Minnesota

Pebble Plus is published by Capstone Press,
151 Good Counsel Drive, P.O. Box 669, Mankato, Minnesota 56002.
www.capstonepress.com

1 2 3 4 5 6 09 08 07 06 05 04

Library of Congress Cataloging-in-Publication Data
Hall, Margaret, 1947–
    Grasshoppers/by Margaret Hall.
    p. cm.—(Pebble plus: Bugs, bugs, bugs!)
    Includes bibliographical references and index.
    ISBN 0-7368-2588-6 (hardcover)
    ISBN 0-7368-5096-1 (paperback)
    1. Grasshoppers—Juvenile literature. [1. Grasshoppers.] I. Title. II. Series.
QL508.A2 H29 2005
595.7′26—dc22   2003024964

Summary: Simple text and photographs describe the physical characteristics and habits of grasshoppers.

Editorial Credits
Sarah L. Schuette, editor; Linda Clavel, series designer; Kelly Garvin, photo researcher; Karen Hieb,
    product planning editor

Photo Credits
Bill Johnson, 6–7
Bruce Coleman Inc./Gary Meszaros, 4–5; Laura Riley, 20–21
David Liebman, 12–13, 16–17
Dwight R. Kuhn, 9, 19
Gerry Ellis & Michael Durham/PictureQuest, 1
Pete Carmichael, 11, 15
Robert & Linda Mitchell, cover

Note to Parents and Teachers

The Bugs, Bugs, Bugs! series supports national science standards related to the diversity of life and heredity. This book describes and illustrates grasshoppers. The images support early readers in understanding the text. The repetition of words and phrases helps early readers learn new words. This book also introduces early readers to subject-specific vocabulary words, which are defined in the Glossary section. Early readers may need assistance to read some words and to use the Table of Contents, Glossary, Read More, Internet Sites, and Index/Word List sections of the book.

Word Count: 84
Early-Intervention Level: 11

Table of Contents

Grasshoppers 4

How Grasshoppers Look 6

What Grasshoppers Do 16

Glossary 22

Read More 23

Internet Sites 23

Index/Word List 24

Grasshoppers

What are grasshoppers?

Grasshoppers are insects.

4

How Grasshoppers Look

Many grasshoppers have
green or brown bodies.
Grasshoppers also can
be other colors.

Grasshoppers are about the size of a child's little finger. Grasshoppers have six legs and two wings.

9

Grasshoppers have two
large eyes.

Grasshoppers have two antennas. Grasshoppers feel and smell with their antennas.

Grasshoppers have two
sharp jaws.

What Grasshoppers Do

Grasshoppers chew and chomp on plants.

Grasshoppers jump.

They use their long

back legs to jump high.

Male grasshoppers rub
their legs against their
wings to sing.

Glossary

antenna—a feeler; insects use antennas to sense movement, to smell, and to listen to each other.

insect—a small animal with a hard outer shell, six legs, three body sections, and two antennas; most insects have wings.

jaw—a part of the mouth used to grab, bite, and chew

male—an animal that can father young

Read More

Allen, Judy, and Tudor Humphries. *Are You a Grasshopper?* Backyard Books. New York: Kingfisher, 2002.

Scholl, Elizabeth J. *Grasshoppers.* Bugs. San Diego: Kidhaven Press, 2004.

Trumbauer, Lisa. *The Life Cycle of a Grasshopper.* Life Cycles. Mankato, Minn.: Pebble Books, 2004.

Internet Sites

FactHound offers a safe, fun way to find Internet sites related to this book. All of the sites on FactHound have been researched by our staff.

Here's how:

1. Visit *www.facthound.com*

2. Type in this special code **0736825886** for age-appropriate sites. Or enter a search word related to this book for a more general search.

3. Click on the **Fetch It** button.

FactHound will fetch the best sites for you!

Index/Word List

against, 20

antennas, 12

bodies, 6

chew, 16

chomp, 16

colors, 6

eyes, 10

feel, 12

insects, 4

jaws, 14

jump, 18

legs, 8, 18, 20

male, 20

plants, 16

rub, 20

sharp, 14

sing, 20

size, 8

smell, 12

wings, 8, 20